Sears Roebuck & Co.

INCORPORATED

SPORTING GOODS DEPARTMENT

WE ARE HEADQUARTERS FOR EVERYTHING IN

Guns, Revolvers, Ammunition, Gun Implements,   Hunters' Clothing, Fishing Tackle,   Lake and River Seines, Tents, Base Ball,   Tennis and other Athletic Goods,

and we can save you money on anything in this line, no matter how little o how much you want to buy.

TERMS

WE WILL SHIP ANY GUN OR REVOLVER TO ANY ADDRESS by Express, C. O. D., subject to examination, on receipt of $1.00 as a guarantee of good faith, and if the goods are exactly as represented, pay the express agent the balance, otherwise return the goods. We would, however, recommend that you send full amount of cash with your order and save the charges collected by all express companies for the return of the C. O. D. money to us. YOU RUN NO RISK by doing this, as all our goods are guaranteed exactly as represented, or your money will be refunded. Guns, rifles, revolvers, etc., made to special order cannot be sent C. O. D.; send cash in full with order

OUR TERMS on FISH NETS and TENTS of all kinds, are Cash in Full with Order, as these goods are made up specially to your order. This does not delay orders, however, as we always fill these orders in three to six days, according to the number of orders we have on hand when we receive your order.

PARKER BREECH LOADING SHOTGUNS

FOR A SPECIAL CONFIDENTIAL PRICE, a much lower price than was ever printed by anyone, A PRICE THAT WILL SURPRISE YOU, Special Terms and our Free Trial Offer, write us, state the grade wanted by number, length of barrel, weight and get OUR SPECIAL OFFER BY RETURN MAIL.

WE OMIT THE PRICE IN THIS CATALOGUE for the reason that the maker objects to our printing a price as low as we can sell these guns; the price would be so much lower than others sell the Parker gun, so much less than you or others ever heard of, that it would demoralize prices and injure the maker's business.

WE CAN WRITE YOU OUR LOWEST PRICE and our special offer if you will only write us for them. We contracted for an immense number of these Parker guns; we got them at the lowest price ever known on condition that we would not print the low price we can sell them at.

WE CAN'T SELL YOU THE PARKER for as little money as a Davis, Remington or Ithaca, but it will cost so little that it will surprise you. The Celebrated Parker needs no lengthy description from anyone. It stands in the front rank of HIGHEST OF HIGH GRADE for twenty-five years. Every Sportsman, every Professional, every Gun Expert knows the Parker Breech Loader as the leader of all American guns.

The above illustration, engraved from a photograph, will give you an idea of the appearance of the NEW IMPROVED MODEL, V. H. GRADE, GENUINE PARKER HAMMERLESS SHOTGUN. Made by Parker Bros., of Meriden, Connecticut. It comes in 12 or 16 gauge, 30 or 32-inch barrel. Finest Vulcan steel barrels; weight of 12-gauge, 7¼ to 8¼ pounds; 2¾ to 3¼ inches drop, finest top lever break, choke bored, imported walnut stock, fancy checkered full pistol grip, handsomely engraved hard rubber butt plate, choke bored by the best known process, to insure the most perfect target, and the greatest possible penetration.

THE PARKER IS MADE OF THE BEST MATERIAL MONEY CAN BUY.

Embodies Every Point of Excellence Known to Gun Making. Every Gun Covered by a BINDING GUARANTEE.

Hammer Guns.

No. 33801   T Grade, twist barrels, extension rib, engraved, American stock, checkered pistol grip and fore end. 12-gauge. List price...$........
No. 33803   It grade, same as No. 33801, 10-gauge. List price.....$........
No. 33805   G grade, Damascus barrels, extension rib, engraved, imported stock, checkered pistol grip and fore end. 12-gauge. Price, $........
No. 33807   E grade, same as No. 33805, 10-gauge. List price.... .....

Weight, 12-gauge, 7¼ to 8¼ pounds; 30 or 32-inch barrels; 10-gauge, 9 to 10 pounds; length of barrel, 30 to 32 inches; 16-gauge, 28 or 30-inch barrels, 8¾ to 7½ pounds. Any deviation from these dimensions is liable to cause delay, and any guns made to special order will cost extra according to amount of extra work required.   Higher Priced Guns made to Special Order.

Hammerless Guns.

No. 33810   D H grade, has very fine Damascus barrels, very fine imported walnut stock, fine checkering and engraving, 12-gauge only. List price....................$........
No. 33812   E H grade, fine Damascus barrels, fine imported stock, nicely engraved. 10-gauge made to special order only. List price$........
No. 33814   G H grade, fine Damascus barrels, fine imported stock, nicely engraved, 12 or 16-gauge. List price.............$........
No. 33816   P H grade, fine English twist barrels, fine American stock, fine engraving, 12 or 16-gauge. List price................$.. ....
No. 33818   V H grade, Vulcan steel barrels, fine American stock, plain frame, made in 12 and 16-gauge only. List price.... ...$........

For a Special Price on any grade of Parker Hammer or Hammerless Guns, a lower price than was ever before quoted, a lower price than the manufacturers will allow us to print, or will allow anyone else to print, and for Special Terms and a Special Free Trial Offer, write us.

DON'T FAIL TO WRITE US BEFORE ORDERING A PARKER GUN, or any other high grade American gun, for you will be surprised the amount of money we can save you. If you are about to buy from your dealer at home or order from some other house, a Baker, Ithaca, Hollenbeck, or other grade American gun of the cheaper class, and you are selecting such a gun because it is among the cheaper grade of guns, first write us, and in all probability we will be able to name you a lower price even on the CELEBRATED GENUINE PARKER GUN than you would pay some one else for one of the cheaper makes.

Our Special Price will be a Net Confidential Price, our Offer a Confidential Offer, and the only condition we make is that you treat it as strictly confidential. This the manufacturer exacts from us in allowing us to name the extraordinary low price.

OUTHOUSES OF THE EAST

PHOTOGRAPHS BY SHERMAN HINES
TEXT BY RAY GUY

NIMBUS PUBLISHING LTD.

To all who have found in the Outhouses of the East places of refuge, utility and meditative serenity this book is dedicated with the hope that it may rekindle their warm interest in an area that has for too long remained but little more than a frozen asset in the treasury of our Atlantic heritage.

Back in the time when we all used them, we seemed hardly to notice them. They were so much a part of everyday life that they blended into the landscape. It was the arrival of indoor plumbing that made the outhouse indecorously comic.

The installation of the first two or three porcelain flushables in a community suddenly swung a spotlight of ridicule on all the old faithful, now old fashioned biffies, for miles around.

A rustic stigma settled over them. The very concept of an outhouse prompted a faint smile, just as ducks do by their mere existence, or signs with the "Rs" printed backwards, or a prolonged prelude to a sneeze or words like "comatose".

You didn't go out of your way to mention that you were no stranger to the proper maintenance and function of the little structures seen now mainly in cartoons in barbershop magazines.

Outhouses, like poor puns, fell out of odor.

But that's all behind us now. The appropriate interval has passed and an affectionate glow of nostalgia has replaced the more unkind spotlight generated by the first flush of indoor china.

From a safe distance, we put the manifold rigors of outhouse usage far to our rear . . . those piercing northeasterly drafts; those creepie crawlies or, far worse, those enraged wingy stingies; the doors that blew open to reveal your private endeavours to the world; the late discovery that not even a catalogue had been provided.

We remember only the happy times. We reflect that, compared to the brutal excesses of modernity, outhouses served their purpose simply, honestly and well.

So you may well think while fumbling for the exact change for the shopping mall or airport cubicle, with the stench of formaldehyde reaming your sinuses and the palpable odor of piped in music curling your ears.

No less intimidating is the private successor to the al fresco privy.

Whisper-flush, Tidy-bol, baby-powder soft, frangipani air freshener, color-coordinated china in "Desert Sand", stained glass illuminations, hanging ferns and twining tendrils, beaming sunlamps and morocco-bound volumes.

Have you entered to perform a bodily function in a place that seems geared for ecstatic religious experience?

Although many of those portrayed within, reek now only of nostalgia, the outhouse still lives throughout the East.

There are two broad categories . . . those of the coast and those of the farmlands. The former is often perched directly above the mighty North Atlantic itself which can humble, if not entirely inhibit the user thereof who meditates too deeply on the puny efforts of Man compared to the awesome works of Nature.

Drafts in these coastal conveniences tend to be more piercing and the structures themselves more rough-hewn than the precisely-crafted domestic appurtenances of the gentler inlands.

In fact, in parts of Cape Breton and Newfoundland the fishing "stage" itself is pressed into dual service, the operative feature being the "trunk hole" or opening in the floor through which fish guts and heads are dumped directly into the sea.

Farley Mowat, in his book "The Boat Who Wouldn't Float", relates the scarifying encounter by dapper Toronto book publisher Jack McClelland with one of these in a Newfoundland outport.

McClelland made the mistake of casting a preliminary glance down through one of these "trunk holes" which was met by the expectant piscatorial gaze of the swarming conners, sculpins and eels below. The spectacle gave him excruciating pause.

Such minor inconveniences have their counterparts inland in the shapes of bulls that choose to doze away a sunny afternoon directly in front of the door or geese that take an aggressive proprietary attitude.

Outhouses have passed through three phases already — taken-for-granted necessaries, objects of rustic stigma, items of nostalgia — and a fourth may be in the wind.

Ecologists, pollution-fighters, the back-to-nature brigade, believe that a step toward the outdoor privy is a step in the right direction.

A brighter gold upon the buttercup and a glorious proof to the keen organic gardener of the "waste-not-want-not" principle. Indeed, the remarkable power of the compost beneath has caused the nearer structure itself to sprout greenery and the further one to produce an infant outhouse from a stalk at its peak.

As idyllic as it gets, with the scent of appleblossom overwhelming any baser odors thus freeing the mind from worry of aresol sprays and destruction of the ozone layer and allowing it to soar in tranquil contemplation. Of course, there are bees. But who said it was an absolutely perfect world?

A cuddlesome number conducive to a leisurely sojourn with the adjacent wall of soft grey shingles hanging like a security blanket. Even the fence is totally relaxed.

Co-operative independence is the prevading spirit here. It sits assertively on its own foundations yet does not shun the protection offered by its neighbors. No frivilous half-moons here, but a four-square gaze suggesting a business-like in-and-out approach.

In the dark of the moon, when the surf moans softly on a distant beach, and only the startled cry of a gull breaks the oppressive silence, an eerie light gleams in the window of the old Foxcroft outhouse. This strange phenomena occurs regularly each month and coincides with the arrival of the Reader's Digest. Old Foxcroft is a slow reader.

Just up the road from old man Foxcroft's is the Baskerville property. Weekend guests are torn between need and unease as they tread their way toward the mouldering convenience through funereal flowers hung with cobwebs. The door swings and squeaks. Bats have been known to burst forth.

A fine example of the "bump-out" style of biffy favored by some industrious farm folk. Personal necessity need not interrupt the daily round of chores. Dobbin's tail misses not a stroke of the curry comb nor Bossy a single squeeze.

Dandelions to some, but still "Piss-a-beds" in many parts of Newfoundland where the old usages of Devon and Cornwall persist. Children are cautioned not to pluck them, as handling them is supposed to cause bed-wetting. But surely, in convenient circumstances like these the gathering of a posy of this potent diuretic is permissable.

A shining example of Maritime craftsman-ship with its fine detailing, careful joinery and solid appearance. A marriage of native materials and native skills. Built for legen-dary permanence but without the mechani-cal coldness of Upper Canadian brick.

Goldenrod and the last mild days of Indian Summer . . . there's a fine melancholy here, a wistful remembrance of those warmer months which allowed unhurried contemplation, solitary philosophizing and leisurely perusal of the catalogue. But soon the thermometer will drop, the north wind will blow and all that will be behind us.

At the first crack of rosy dawn, the Eastern fisherman is away to plow the deeps. He will shortly emerge after his morning ablutions, lower the ladder from the clifftop and descend to the shoreline. Or it may just be there in case of fire.

The thoughts of those who live by, on and from the sea are never far from the sea. But never closer than here. This model located directly above the teeming waters boasts a bamboo fishing rod kept always to hand on the fence. You replace it there when you come out.

Barn door hex marks are still a common sight in some areas. Circles, hearts, squares and other painted shapes are supposed to protect the cattle and horses against colic, glanders, staggers, heaves, miscarriages and other calamities. The diamond on the privy door helps prevent asphixiation, faulty range, and mistaken double occupancy.

Change and decay in all around we see . . . but the basic necessity is maintained. The barn's sagging, leaking and boarded up but the outhouse sports new asphalt shingles, vertical plank siding, sash trim and maybe a new fangled roll as soft as dandelion fluff.

A communal effort with convenient hand-rails for use in raging blizzards, dense fog and by the near-sighted. The door is kept co-operatively open and an equal-time use schedule strictly enforced. Long life to the glorious people's privy. As someone has said, "The East is Red".

A fine example of the more rugged style of coastal architecture as compared to the more delicately-finished and detailed structures found inland. No frills here. Even the approach ramp has been kept to the minimum of a single plank. Yet this honest pile is sturdy enough to defy the elements, stand firmly against an 80-knot gale . . .

. . . then along came an 81-knot gale. The most romantic perhaps, of our collection is this old sea-dog W.C. cast ashore apparently by the tides of fortune with the flotsom and jetsam. Its door, bearing no half-moon but a triangle, was last seen still adrift off Bermuda.

There are 18,753 blossoms on this old apple tree. To every five blossoms there is a busy bee. Even the busiest bee must rest now and then, hence the conveniently-placed rest room. A resting bee, if roused, gets riled . . . so, thank you very much, I'll grin and bear it to the outskirts of apple country.

Kept on as a pet after indoor plumbing put it out to pasture. Why not? A museum, perhaps, to the past glories of detached lavitoria, restored strictly to period in shingles and the 1948 Fall and Winter edition of Eaton's mailorder catalogue, antique quicklime box and an upper denture never claimed. Lovingly maintained by the local Preserve Our Old Privies chapter.

Sensibly braced against the invigorating westerlies which hurl themselves across the icy bay to cruely buffet its underpinnings, this coastal outhouse stands fast and on the job. Its patrons would be wise to take similar precautions against the rigorous natural ventilation. Nothing less than four fingers of overproof Demarrera is recommended.

Body and spirit cringe in the face of so harsh and inhumane a prospect. The distance to be travelled, the complete lack of shelter, the prevading chilled-corpse genius of the architect. Only a homesick Siberian or a disciple of an extreme religious sect devoted to mortification of the flesh could have conceived such a monstrosity.

Ducks dawdle daintily down delightful dandelion-dotted declivity discretely distaining dilapidated domicile doubtless debauching divers dreadful decency-defiling downdrafts downgrading district.

With today's rising effluence, more and more families boast a two-privy residence. Here we have our choice of, to the left, cool and cold running water depending on the season, solar heating, natural ventilation and other mod cons and, to the right, an unrivaled marine vista with a 30-foot drop to the beach in case of a wrong left turn on emerging.

Thoughtfully provided for the fairies at the bottom of this garden is the dinky number listed in the catalogue as "Toadstool Tidy — Model B." The wee folk, though more accustomed to a pot of gold, do appreciate this sort of consideration. The diminutive occupant right now has tethered his mount, standing barely two hands high, to the rail.

Here is what you call your classic approach-avoidance conflict. Many minutes — which seem like hours — are spent in psychological turmoil in the face of such a situation. But finally the need to approach can so overwhelm the tendency to avoid that the bull is taken by the horns.

"Disgraceful, that's what I call it! With all the money they've spent. My dear, the lineups weren't as bad as this when we were at Expo '67."

As we move closer to the seat of the matter, some heartwarming details emerge. At top, there's weatherstripping (a humanitarian touch) plus a new window cut in the door low enough to provide a view when seated. Center, so tender a touch of the craftsman's hand as you could wish with never a cruel edge or a sharp corner. Bottom, if the groove in the wood below the latch was worn by the hook as it swung in the wind . . . then occupancy time here must have spanned ages.

An outhouse by any other name . . . Is this a concession to modernity and visitors from town? Thoughtful, perhaps, but bound to mislead. Of course, you can point out to them that they don't always go into a bathroom to bathe, either.

Signs that if the young and mischievious at heart can take to the outhouse with such glee it may indeed be due for a revival. With youth converted to the cause, there'll be a sigh of relief from the old traditionalists who've long fought a lonely rear-guard action.

Surely a non-functional model that just sits there looking pretty for the tourists cameras, lace curtain in the window and all. As with icebergs, the major part of an outhouse lies beneath the surface. Yet this one is perched on solid granite and so must be a counterfeit. Should its bluff be called, a tour guide has to scamper around to the rear and slip in a sheet of tinfoil? I lose my bet if it has a dynamited basement.

Utter tranquility of mind is afforded by this wallpapered privy. The restful pattern of leaves and flowers, the homey calm of the design . . . and the knowledge that you need never be threatened here by the trauma of the missing roll.

Surely, there can be no more charming adjunct to the well-appointed privy than a nest of singing birds. What a delight to sit and gaze upwards in rapt contemplation as the little feathered creatures go about their daily . . . Whoops! How about an in-house outhouse for birds?

Produced by Nimbus Publishing Limited
3731 MacKintosh St., Halifax, N.S., Canada.

Designed by Nancy Margeson

Color Separations and Phototypesetting by
Maritime Photoengravers Ltd., Halifax, N.S.

Printed and bound by Everbest printing Co Ltd in Hong Kong

Special thanks from Sherman Hines to:

Isabel Macneill who first suggested photographing and documenting this fast
disappearing once essential part of our landscape.

All Maritimers' who allowed me to photograph their "privies" and those who don't
know I did!

Bruce Law

Camera and Film used:
Pentax 6 × 7 $2^1/_4 \times 2^3/_4$
Ektachrome

First impression — West House Publishing Ltd. 1978
   ISBN 0-969052-01-4

Second impression — Nimbus Publishing Limited 1979
   ISBN 0-920852-03-3

Third impression— Nimbus Publishing Limited 1981
   ISBN 0-920852-03-3

Fourth impression—Nimbus Publishing Limited 1985
   ISBN 0-920852-03-3

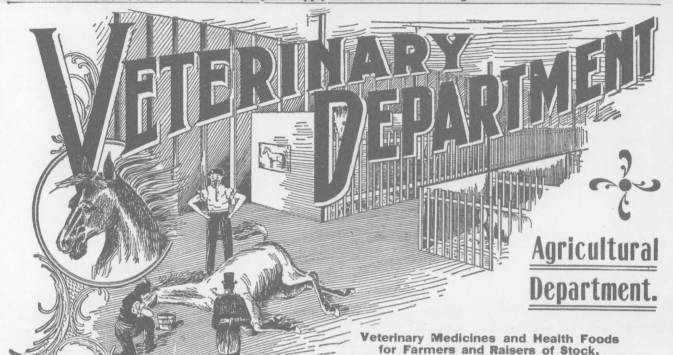

VETERINARY DEPARTMENT

Agricultural Department.

Veterinary Medicines and Health Foods for Farmers and Raisers of Stock.

....KEEP YOUR ANIMALS HEALTHY AND SAVE MONEY AND WORRY....

WE PRESENT TO OUR CUSTOMERS a most valuable and complete line of internal and external remedies and health foods for horses, cattle, sheep, hogs, poultry, dogs, and all domestic animals. These have been carefully selected by our Veterinary Surgeon and we guarantee them to be the best preparations of this kind ever offered to the farmer and raiser of stock. You can thoroughly rely on what we say concerning each of them. When your animals are sick and out of condition give these remedies a trial. You will be surprised with the good results. Your animals will soon become well again and feel in better condition than ever. You will find enclosed with each package, complete instructions how to use these remedies, and also valuable information how to treat sick animals.

Veterinary Blister.

A Good Blister for Animals is a Rare and Valuable Article.

We have spent much time and made many experiments in preparing a really practical and thoroughly reliable blister that can be applied easily, and good results follow. We have submitted samples to the best veterinary surgeons in the country and they have approved of it, and are using it daily in their practice. It is unexcelled for bone spavin, ring bone, splint, curb, bog spavin, blood spavin, thoroughpin, etc. Removes wind puffs, calouses, etc., from kicks and bruises, thickening of tendons, etc. Full information how to use it and a description of bone spavin, etc., with each package.

No. 5750 Each 40c
If by mail, postage extra, per box, 8 cents.

ACME VETERINARY BLISTER SOLD ONLY BY SEARS ROEBUCK AND COMPANY INC CHICAGO ILL.

Veterinary Fattening Powder.

If your horse is out of condition and getting thin, give him two tablespoonfuls of this powder morning and night, and in a few days he will look like a new animal so that your neighbor will scarcely know him.

ACME VETERINARY FATTENING CONDITION POWDERS SOLD ONLY BY SEARS ROEBUCK & CO INC CHICAGO ILL.

Give your cows a dose with each feed of grain, meal or chopped stuff, dampened with water. You will be surprised at the large increase and improvement in quality of the milk as well as the better condition of the animal. Calves, sheep and cattle of all kinds improve in flesh and health when the powder is used occasionally. It is the very best fattening and health giving powder in the market. We guarantee its qualities to our customers. Use this remedy in time; do not wait until your stock is sick, but give it to ward off sickness. It pays for itself, keeping the animal in a strong, healthy condition.

No. 5752 10 lb. package .... $1.00   25 lb. package $2.00
           50 lb. package .... 3.50   100 lb. package 6.00

Veterinary Fever Remedy.

Give in all diseases that are accompanied by fever. Give early in lung fever, pneumonia, bronchitis, pleurisy, laryngitis, sore throat, distemper, cold, etc. It is a positive cure, if given promptly, in an attack of laminitis, or founder, and accompanied by hot poultices to the horse's feet, it will remove the congestion and effect a permanent cure in a few hours. In case of inflammation of the bowels, given with Acme Colic Cure, and hot applications to the belly, gives relief to the patient and cures the disease in a few hours.

No. 5756 Bottle, each 40c
Unmailable account of weight.

ACME VETERINARY FEVER REMEDY SOLD ONLY BY SEARS ROEBUCK AND CO. INC. CHICAGO ILL.

Veterinary Wire Cut Remedy.

This is a remedy which should always be within reach. It is worth many times its cost when wanted.

It will heal cuts and wounds in all parts of the body without leaving a scar. It is the best remedy for cuts from barbed wire; it heals them the quickest. In using this remedy it is not necessary to sew any cuts! If you have a flap that hangs down, fasten it in place by a bandage, but don't close the sore—give it a free chance to discharge. By applying this remedy it will soon heal. It is an antiseptic destroying all germs and foul odors. It also preserve the sores from flies and insects.

No. 5760 Price, per bottle 40c
Unmailable on account of weight.

ACME VETERINARY WIRE CUT REMEDY SOLD ONLY BY SEARS ROEBUCK AND CO. INC. CHICAGO ILL.

Acme Veterinary Cough Powder.

A sure cure for all coughs, colds, distemper, laryngitis, pneumonia, pleurisy, etc. Full instructions for use with description of the symptoms of distemper on each package.

No. 5764 Price, per box 25c

If by mail, postage extra, 8 cents.

GALL CURE PRICE 25 Cts. TRADE MARK CHICAGO USA

Gall Cure.

A gall cure that can be depended upon. It will heal collar galls, hit galls, saddle galls, boot galls, and abrasions of the skin, while the animal is at work. Toughens the skin, stains the parts and makes a galled horse look respectable. Quickest cure, most economical and humane treatment.

No. 5766 Per box 25c

If by mail, postage extra, 4 cents.